Essential Self Defence
Basic Advice for Men, Women & Children

Written by Andy Crittenden

Introduction
Why am I writing this book?
Depends on the tone depends on the answer.

So, the reason I have decided to write this book is I feel like I should give something back, to who I don't know, I would suggest that this book be aimed at people with little or no knowledge of Self Defence and no formal Self Defence training. However, I hope it can be useful to anyone regardless of background, experience or knowledge. With an open mind, you might just learn one thing that could help you one day.

If you ask the question in another tone, the reason I am writing this book is for the last 20 years I have studied Self Defence under the watchful eye of Dave Turton, highly regarded as one of the world's leading authorities. I also have 34 years of Martial Arts experience under my belt, training with many different Master's in a variety of Martial Arts.

Now let's get this straight, there are lots of more qualified people than me to write a book on Self Defence and if they have written one then good luck to them and however if they have not, I hope you enjoy my take on it.

I'm not going to say I was a doorman or came from a life of crime or anything like that, I am just a normal guy who learnt from the best and taught Self Defence for many years at my School with my regular long term students where we tested the methods I had been taught and also have taught many different groups on short courses and they say teaching is learning twice and that's very true especially when it comes to teaching Self Defence often to groups that do not want to be there.

In my life I have only had around a dozen street conflicts, none of which I would call a fight. What I can say in all humility that in all these situations I have come away relatively unscathed and only ever used basic techniques to get me home safe.

There will be nothing flashy or difficult to learn in this book, just pure basics with an emphasis on getting out of the situation you are in and get home safe.

The advice is often to run, which is great but where are you running too? Can you guarantee that the person or people attacking you cannot outrun you? So yes, run but put yourself in a better position to get away first.

I hope that you enjoy reading this book as much as I enjoyed writing it, remember this is literally what I would teach on an Introduction to Self Defence course, to make this material work you should enrol on a course or in a class, my goal for this book is that it sparks an interest in people who take up Self Defence, the more people who can defend themselves the better.

About the Author

Andy Crittenden has trained in Martial Arts since the age of 7, at the age of 19 he decided he wanted to add Self Defence skills to his Training and sought out the Number 1 Self Defence Instructor in the UK Dave Turton.

Andy enjoyed the lessons with Dave and his right-hand man Karl Blackwell eventually attaining a Black Belt in Dave's SDF Modern Street Combat system, from there he studied Goshinkwai under Dave and as of writing is a 5th Dan Black Belt, one of only a few people to attain this rank from Dave.

When Dave formulated his Self Defence Instructor Diploma's Andy was amongst the first to attain the rank of Master Level Instructor and then one of the first Assessors meaning he could train other Instructor's and finally one of only a handful of people to be awarded the level of Master Assessor meaning he could now train other Assessors.

Andy is the Founder of ACMAC Martial Arts which have Schools in Yorkshire, Nottinghamshire & Derbyshire, he is the Founder of the Multi Skilled Martial Arts system and holds the rank of 7th Degree Black Belt plus additional Black Belts in Tae Kwon Do, Kick Boxing, Eskrima, Ju-Jitsu and as previously mentioned Goshinkwai/SDF Modern Street Combat.

He is also the Lead Self Defence Instructor from Alliance Martial Arts & Self Defence Association and has taught Self Defence all over the UK and Ireland to Martial Artists and non Martial Artists.

He is considered an expert in the field.

Acknowledgements

I have had many influences in the Martial Arts and in the Self Defence aspects of training. The Senior Black Belts when I started Goshinkwai all were a great help, nothing was too much especially if they got to show me one more time and inflict some pain on me or the person I was training with. Joe Turton (Dave's dad) was still training well into his 70's and I thought no matter how hard the class was I couldn't stop as he was smashing everything in front of him. The other big influence was Karl Blackwell who was there on my very first lesson and threw me around like a rag doll & made me realise I needed to learn this stuff.

I have had some great training partners over the years in Self Defence and I appreciate anyone who has trained with me over the year. My main training partner has been Ian Harrison, we have trained together for almost 20 years and pushed each other to be better students, I could not have wished for anyone better to spend Tuesday mornings with, it was a life changing decision to train together under the great Mr Turton.

I have had a few other Instructors who have taught me Self Defence outside of Goshinkwai/SDF that have influenced me include Andrew Morrell of the CMAA in Manchester and the Bolton Iron Man Trevor Roberts, who I have learnt a lot from on this aspect, the second most influential Self Defence Instructor that I have had. Of course, if this was about Martial Arts it would be a much longer list.

My own Black Belts at ACMAC Martial Arts have inspired and motivated me to be the best I can be, especially the Goshinkwai/SDF Black Belts. I am blessed to have some excellent long-term students, 15, 20 & 25 years of dedication, loyalty and friendship is something very special.

My main influence has of course been Dave Turton, he has been biggest influence in Self Defence by far, he has taught me 99% of Self Defence and much of this book is from his teachings, I could not have found a better Instructor who became a great mentor and a close friend. I would not have written this book without his blessing.

My family have always been supportive of me especially my Wife Lucy who has to put up with me and all my crazy obsessions with Martial Arts and Self Defence and provides the love and support I need to make me the best version of myself, my step Daughters Ebony & Tiff who gave me motivation to be the best I can be when they came into my life many years ago, my Dad supports me in everything I do in life and in Martial Arts and my Mum is my inspiration, everything I do is to make her proud.

During the writing of this book I got a massive writers block which hit me for around 4 months because I used to read each chapter to my dogs Rocco & Billy every night and we lost Billy while I was deep into the Ladies Self Defence section, it took me a while to pick the pen back up, but I'm glad I did,

Apart from the first two photos, last two photos and one in the middle, all the others that appear in this book all were taken at photo shoots at ACMAC Martial Arts in Balby with a few of the Instructors & Students all taken by Alastair Bell of Alastair Bell Photography.

The 2nd one is a very special as it features one of my Black Belts Sophie Hawkins being followed by two great guys both of whom are sadly no longer with us, first of all her dad Steve Hawkins who was a great guy and volunteered to be in this photo even though he didn't train and the other a close friend of mine Martin McAteer known to us all as Macca who was a big part of the Self Defence scene at my School as a Self Defence Instructor & SDF Black Belt. Both very much missed. This photo was for a Self Defence course I was running.

Thank you to Stefan Johnson, Lucy Crittenden, Tiff Richardson, Jordan Rowe, Kelly Ashbridge, Cieran Ashbridge, Mick Woodhall, Jamie Hunter, Brandon Hunter, Oscar Snedker, George Snedker, Heidi Sunderland, Amelia Bell & Mescha Benson for being in the photos and bringing this book to life.

Finally, I want to thank Gary Henderson of Martial Arts Creative for designing the cover of this book.

Foreword by David Turton 10th Dan

Over the decades that l have been involved in the realms of self-defence there have been numerous books, articles films and DVD's, most with a similar 'fee'.

So why do l feel this one has an edge over many others? Well first because Andy Crittenden is a genuine 5th Dan Black Belt in the art of self-defence as well as his many other qualifications, and secondly because it offers a genuinely honest approach and look self-defence.

The first clue is its title ESSENTIAL, and this is important, Andy isn't trying to promote a specific or particular martial arts style but is offering a sensible view of the subject which is valid for everyone.

I have known Andy for around 25 years when he first came to me as a student of my methods when he was already a holder of black belts in other martial arts. He eventually became a top student, a close friend and often accompanied me all around the UK on my teaching seminars.

He gained black belts in my system eventually reaching a 5th Dan black bet at the time of writing this foreword. As well as teaching other martial arts at his clubs in Doncaster, Andy also has a separate class for my system at his school. I have to say he has produced many excellent students, many also making black belts in self-defence.

This book is well written and easily readable and digested and is written by an author you can trust and be assured really knows his subject.

If you never buy or read another book on Self Defence, buy and read THIS one... highly recommended indeed, and l have spent over SIXTY years studying this subject.
Make it a vital part of your book collection... ESSENTIAL SELF DEFENCE is essential reading.

David Turton 10th Dan

Pic 1 – Andy Crittenden & Dave Turton

Chapters List

Introduction

Section 1 – Basic Adult Self Defence
Chapter 1 - Confidence   15
Chapter 2 - Awareness, Avoidance & Escape   17
Chapter 3 – Self Protection   19
Chapter 4 – The Law & Self Defence   21
Chapter 5 – Power Talking   23
Chapter 6 – Emotions & Colour Code   25
Chapter 7 – Blocks & Releases   27
Chapter 8 - Control the Distance, Control the Fight   31
Chapter 9 - Time must be on your side   33
Chapter 10 - The Fence & The Guard   35
Chapter 11 - The Basic Strikes & Best Targets   37
Chapter 12 - Training for Power, Accuracy & Timing   51
Chapter 13 - Grappling Techniques   55
Chapter 14 - Expedient Weapons   61
Chapter 15 - Defences against 10 common attacks   63

Section 2 – Specific Ladies Self Defence
Chapter 16 – Difference in Women's Self Defence   77
Chapter 17 - A Woman's best Weapons   79
Chapter 18 - Advice on Domestic Violence   85
Chapter 19 - Dealing with Unwanted Attention   87
Chapter 20 - Sexual Assaults   89

Section 3 – Children's Self Defence
Chapter 21 - Building Confidence & Skills   97
Chapter 22 - Techniques all Children should know   99
Chapter 23 - School Fights   119
Chapter 24 - Dealing with Bullying   127
Chapter 25 - Stranger Danger   131

Final Thoughts & Afterword   139

Section 1
Basic Adult Self Defence

Chapter 1
Confidence

The first thing I would say to you is that people who have Self Confidence are often less likely to be targeted. This can be like the Chicken and the Egg as often Self Confidence comes from the ability to Defend yourself, so whilst you build your Self Defence skills its important you work on your confidence too.

You can portray Self Confidence by your Body Language, being able to hold your head high and walk and talk with confidence could be a quick way out of a dangerous situation.

It is not that simple of course; I suppose you can fake it till you make it but not everyone has that mindset.

So, it is something that I think you would have to train into yourself over a long period of time, walk with confidence, talk with confidence and act confidently even when you don't feel Confident. Eventually it will catch on or at least improve with time.

People look for those who are walking with their head down, who can not make eye contact, who have a weak handshake and can't hold a conversation with new people they meet.

Do not allow yourself to be the person people look at and label VICTIM.

Your Confidence is your shield, but even the most confident people can still be targeted and attacked it's just less likely.

Chapter 2
Awareness, Avoidance & Escape

These are your first line of defence and the best way to keep yourself out of trouble, being aware of what is going off, avoiding situations and being able to escape if necessary are the most sensible options in Self Defence.

Self-Awareness is very important. If you know there is a pub that has a bad reputation then don't go in it, if you know that a certain area has bad crime then don't drive through it, if you know that an alleyway or subway has gangs hanging around then take the long route.

If you are out and you start to see conflict or loud aggression being projected, move on, go somewhere else, do not get caught in the crossfire.

Avoiding conflict is the best form of Self Defence, if someone asks you what you are looking at you basically have two options.

Option 1 is to escalate things by saying that you are looking at them or give them a clever comment as a comeback.

We are going to spend more time on Option 2 which is to casually say something along the lines of "I was looking at that behind you" or "didn't we go to school or work together" nothing is guaranteed, this is a constant theme in Self Defence however it greatly reduces your chances of conflict by going with option 2 over option 1.

Being aware of Escape routes if you are in a dangerous situation can be very beneficial and increase your chances of getting home safely.

Always take time to check your surroundings when you are in unfamiliar territory. Don't back yourself against a wall or box yourself in.

Escape is not a coward's way out it is a sensible option.

Chapter 3
Self-Protection

Self-Protection to me is the non-physical side of Self Defence, it's the equivalent of someone who suffers with Hay fever taking an antihistamine every day. It's the things you do to Protect yourself from confrontations.

Here are a few examples.

Phones: Say what you want about Mobile Phones, they are a great Self Protection device. Make sure if you are out and about it is fully charged and you have the funds to make calls. Have a Favourites list or Speed Dials to ring the important people in your life easily. If you ever feel like you are being followed ring someone straight away, tell them where you are. They are also pretty good makeshift Weapons, but we will get to that later.

Always tell people where you are going and who you will be with. Make sure someone knows if you are going somewhere a far or somewhere you don't normally go, you don't have to tell everyone just someone you live with, if you live alone just a quick text to say that you are going shopping in Liverpool with Kenny, Robbie & Stevie so I won't be in till later means that the person you text will know where to look for you and who to contact if they cannot get in touch with you.

Don't be on your own, always try and be with someone, if you are out on a night don't walk home or get in a taxi on your own unless you can't avoid it. Stay with your group, stay where its busy. If it's in the daytime stay where its well-lit.

When you are out in public be aware of your surroundings, be careful where you sit, make sure you don't have you back to the door or to a busy part of the pub, restaurant or wherever you are. Keep a tab on behaviour of the other people in the room, if you feel there is a bad atmosphere, it's time to go.

When we go to bed on a night, we make sure that our doors are locked in the house, treat your life in the same way. When you are in your car if you can lock your doors. If you are out and about don't flash your cash or leave your valuables on show. This reduces the risk of being targeted for an attack.

Pic 2 – Female being followed talking on the phone

Chapter 4
The Law & Self Defence

Before we move forward it is important that we understand the Law when it comes to Self Defence.

The Law in Great Britain uses the term Reasonable Force, this means that if taken to court you can explain your actions to be in Self Defence.

Reasonable Force can be different depends on the individuals involved. It can be explained easily with this next sentence, if a 9-year-old girl is attacked by a fully grown man and she grabs a pair of scissors and strikes him, it could be deemed Reasonable Force however if it's the man who grabs the scissors no court in the land would see that as reasonable.

So, whatever you do you must be able to justify in court and also morally in your own mind, many people have had mental health issues from situations that escalated out of control. If you stamp on someone's head you could kill someone when it may not have been necessary when the same move done on the ankle would mean a broken ankle which would mean you have less chance of being up for murder and you would still have a great chance of getting back home safe as they would not be able to run very fast with a broken ankle.

It is often said that you should not hit first, this is not what the law says, would anyone like to give Tyson Fury or Katie Taylor the first shot? No, me neither. You can use a pre-emptive strike if you feel it is needed, if that person is grabbing you, pushing you or being verbally aggressive towards you then the fight has started in their head and this is where you can perform a pre-emptive strike, but remember you must be able to justify this, a single pre-emptive and escape is far more likely to be considered Self Defence than multiple strikes where the opponent does not physically attack back.

Yes, this is all common sense but must be addressed before we move forward. However, I must quote a saying I picked up from Dave Turton which is better to be tried by 12 than carried by 6. There is so many different situations that you can find yourself in ranging from a work mate who can't handle his drink getting a bit aggressive to someone dragging you down an alley who is armed with a Knife. So, it's important you make your decisions based on the situation that you are in.

Chapter 5
Power Talking

This could well be the most important chapter of this book. If you can master the art of Power Talking, you can massively increase your chances of talking your way out of a situation.

There are 3 types of Communication, they are Vocabulary, Tonality & Body Language. The words you say can be interpreted differently depends on how you say it, the tone of your voice can dictate how the words "what are you looking at" can be taken in different way, in a softly spoken voice it can be a question, with an angry tone it's enough to start a fight.

A good exercise is the say that phrase in different tones of voice and with different body language.

Leave me alone said with confidence and strong body language can be enough to make someone think twice about starting an altercation

Pic 3 - Hands up looking passive but using words to calm the assailant down

Chapter 6
Emotions & The Colour Code

Effective Self Defence is very much down to emotion and how you handle it, the Colour Code is important as it prepares you for the emotions that are coming.

There are 4 colours in the Colour Code

White means you totally relaxed in a safe environment, maybe at home with your doors Locked

Yellow means you are in a reasonably safe place, possibly work, where you are comfortable but your still in public and surrounded by others.

Orange your starting notice signals, aggressive behaviour, loud noises etc. This could be time to exit.

Red is fight or flight, the aggression and noise you heard is now aimed at you and you must take action.

You can move through the Colour Code very quickly, for example you are in White state at home Chilled watching a movie the doors are locked, you hear a knock on the door you immediately become Yellow, how many times has this happened and you have said out loud who is this knocking at this time.

To go to Orange you must be in Yellow so let's use that same scenario but this time instead of a knock on the door you hear something in the Garden, you go from White to Yellow pretty quick, then as you are listening you start to move into Orange when you start thinking of your next move.

If you go to where the noise was and maybe grab something to aid you in your defence you are solidly in Orange, the trigger to Red will be to actually see someone or hopefully if you don't see someone you will start moving back into Yellow, it will take some time to go back to White as you will be conscious that you did hear something earlier.

White is a rare state, at home with doors and windows locked is really the only time you should be in White, Yellow is where you should be always aware of what is happening around you.

You will nervous, you will be scared, it is natural you have to control the Fear and Adrenaline you will get when the situation arises.

Remember this a book on Basic Self Defence, if you want to get deeper into this side of things you do not have to look far for some great reads, I am happy to recommend some great Authors to you.

Chapter 7
Blocks & Releases

There isn't a lot of good blocks or necessary blocks. You only need blocks if someone is striking you, movement is the best defence, it's hard to hit a moving target. If you need to block here are the best one's dependant on the strikes.

If someone throws a Swinging Punch to your head which is the most used attack you must step into the arch of the arm with one leg in front of the other and both arms up to protect your head but must not negatively affect your view. The block comes from your strong stance and comes from your feet and legs this provides the base you need to block the attack. This is called the Smother Block.

The other block is a Cover Block, this comes from a straight punch and requires you to step off and you almost salute, it deflects the punch more than meeting it head on like the previous block.

If they are not striking you then they are Grabbing you, depends on the grab depends on the release. The simple principle is to put them in a weaker position than what they were, people grab from strong positions, this can be easily manipulated with the right knowledge.

You can also strike the arm that is grabbing you or if you are convinced the situation cannot be de-escalated then you can strike your way out of the situation.

Here are a few examples against popular attacks.

Pic 4 - Smother Block

Pic 5 - Cover Block

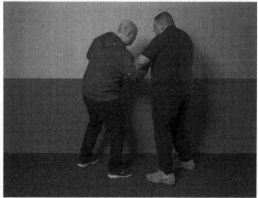

Pic 6 - Strike the Arm to release lapel grab

Pic 7 - Strike the Arm to release throat grab

Pic 8 - Strike the Hand to release under arm bear hug

Pic 9 - Palm Strike to face from Collar Grab

41

Chapter 8
Control the Distance, Control the Fight

This is a book to itself; in this chapter I will go over the basics of
Controlling the distance of the Fight. The theme of this book is to give
Basic advice and encourage the reader to take regular lessons. It is very
difficult to describe in a book but could not be omitted from a book on
Self Defence.

By controlling the distance, you can control the Fight easier. The age
old saying that the best Self Defence is running is a great example of
controlling the distance, if you can run like Usain Bolt then that's great
but there are other ways to control distance.

If you are wishing to diffuse a situation simply stepping back out of
range can mean you have more bargaining time, you can often see the
situation better and assess if this person is alone or is part of a group. If
there are multiple attackers controlling the distance is even more
important.

Obviously it also has offensive advantages, if you can put the correct
distance between yourself and your attacker you can dictate when the
first strike happens, as we said earlier performing a Pre-Emptive strike
is ok in the right situation, if the attacker is coming at you aggressively
and you can hit them on the half step while they are unbalanced will
give you a far greater advantage than hitting someone when they are in
a good stance, its often the surprise shots the finish Professional Fights
such as MMA or Boxing and on the street it is no different.

Pic 10 - Stepping back assessing the situation

Chapter 9
Time must be on your side

So, what does control time mean? The easy understanding of this for Basic level Self Defence is that you control when the fight starts and finishes.

If your attacker is adamant on become violent with you then you may have no other option than to become violent yourself, often they will be verbally aggressive first and the words they are using are usually an indication of how imminent the attack is, to get a Pre-Emptive strike in and control the time of the start of the altercation you can simply just ask them to repeat themselves such as "what did you say mate?" And then you can get your first strike in, create some distance between you and make your escape.

Like I said earlier, just taking time to diffuse the situation means you could ultimately control the timing of the fight by diffusing it completely.

If this book inspires you to start Self Defence training, then there are lots of ways to improve your chances of survival mid fight by using Timing to your advantage but for this book we are looking at dictating when the fight starts and putting you at an advantage from the start.

Pic 11 - Hitting on the Half step

Chapter 10
The Fence & The Guard

These are often the last line of Defence. Often these two moves are confused and merged.

The best way to differentiate the two is that the Fence is an invisible barrier, there isn't any contact other than for a split second, whereas the guard is a physical barrier.

Both may look the same, with your arm out between you and your attacker and one leg back in stance.

The Fence can be mobile as the attacker moves around it, you can move the fence to maintain the distance, by doing this you can dictate when or if the fight starts like we said in the earlier chapters.

One of the benefits of using the Fence or Guard is that it gives you an understanding of range, if the attacker makes contact with your hand, it means you can strike them.

Pic 12 - The Fence

Pic 13 - The Guard

Chapter 11
The Basic Strikes & Best Targets

The best thing you can do initially when learning Self Defence is learn how to hit hard and where to hit.

At first you will not get to grips with Grappling skills to a point that you are comfortable using them when needed but striking is different, you can learn to hit hard from the start and here are some of the strikes we use in our Self Defence system.

The best phrase I can give you is Move Hit Move. A moving target is much harder to hit, or grab hold of, plus you can generate great power this way.

Palm Strike

The first technique I want to discuss is the Palm Strike, make sure your fingers are pulled back, so the striking point is dominant. To create power in any strike it comes from the stance, the power transfers from your feet through your body into you palm. Your desired target is the nose (there are other targets but for Basic Defence lets stick to one target).

When you hit the nose the eyes water, if you can't see you can't fight and that gives you time to plan your next move.

Pic 14 - Palm strike against grabbing attack   Pic 15 - Full Body showing stance

Hammer Fist

The reason we recommend a Hammer fist over a punch is simple, with a hammer fist you hit with the bottom part of the fist, now if you hit a wall with the bottom part of your fist and with the same power punch the same wall you will feel the difference for yourself. Striking with the bottom of the fist won't break your hand as easy as a punch which means you can throw more strikes and still be able to use your hand to grab. The Hammer fist is a natural movement just like hammering something into a wall, hence the name.

Now if you are a Boxer, Kick Boxer, Karateka etc then Punching will be natural to you and you may be more conditioned and you may be quite good at it so go right ahead.

This is a closer range strike and works best especially for Beginners just coming straight down onto the attacker's nose.

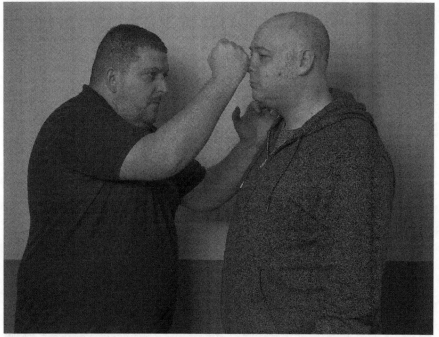

Pic 16 - Hammer fist landing on nose

Pic 17 - Example of how to set up the Hammer fist with a question

The Power Slap

No don't skip this gents, it's not just for Women. This is signature strike of Dave Turton, trust me, I have had this numerous times and seen the biggest bruisers turn believers very quick.

It's actually a cupped hand strike and is the best target is under the ear.

Pic 18 - Power Slap against lapel grab

Pic 19 - Close up of the Slap and Target

Elbow Strike

The Elbow is one of the strongest bones in your body, it is important you understand the strengths and weaknesses of using an Elbow Strike.

The only real weakness is range, you can't throw a good elbow from far away, it's purely a close-range attack. You don't have a great range of movement as it's a shorter distance between your shoulder and elbow than a hand technique which has lots of range of movement.

But that's it, it is a great powerful strike, nice and compact and will do a great amount of damage wherever it lands.

There are a variety of Elbow Strikes you can utilise but for this level we are focusing on a Basic straight Elbow strike

Pic 20 - Elbow Strike from Smother Block

Knee Strikes

Much like Elbow's knee strikes don't have a lot of movement and range but slightly more than elbows. Just like Elbow's they are also extremely dangerous close range and very strong bones. You can use a Knee Strike as a single technique or part of a clinch. A clinch can give you more open targets however it takes away the element of surprise.

Against a Standing opponent there are two main knee strikes, rising knee and round knee. A rising knee would target the groin, thigh or stomach (if you are taller than your attacker), to get a knee to the stomach against a taller opponent you would utilise the clinch, you could also go to the head from the clinch. To reduce the risk of your leg being grabbed tuck your knee in tight so the opponent can't grab behind as easy.

Round knees would go towards the thigh and also the ribs with the same conditions as the rising knee to the stomach, if you have a height advantage the ribs are usually available without clinch, against a taller opponent or even someone of even height as yourself utilising the clinch and pulling them in will aid you reaching your desired target.

If you have managed to get your opponent on the Ground, you can drop a knee to their calf or ankle which would give you a greater chance of escaping, dropping a knee to the head or ribs could get you a prison sentence there for the leg is a better target and still gets you home safe.

Pic 21 - Close range knee to the Groin   Pic 22 - Clinch & Knee

Kicks

Kicks are your longest Weapons on your body, if done correctly can be devastating and effective. Unlike most Martial Arts systems kicks for Self Defence are mainly done below the waist.

Now in my Martial Arts Schools I have some amazing Kickers who can apply head kicks well for the street and if that is you then go for it. Much like I said we would encourage Boxers to Punch in the street as they have those skills, but this book is not aimed at those guys, its aimed at someone who has no experience and wants some tips to defend themselves.

So, we are going to discuss just 5 kicks, the first 3 are the Basic 3 kicks of most Martial Arts Systems applied for the street, the 4th is similar to a Side footer in Football and the 5th being a Stamp. Again, Targets are important

These kicks are more from European Systems (English & French) than Oriental Arts, not for any other reason other than they are Shod whereas most Oriental Kicks are barefoot.

Kick Number 1 is Front Kick, this can be thrown to the Groin as a swing or to the inside of the Thigh as a thrust, the latter being especially effective if one or both of you are grabbing.

Pic 23 - Swinging Front Kick to the Groin

Pic 24 - Grab and Thrust kick to Inside of the thigh

The 2nd kick is the side kick, this is best targeted to the back of the knee and involves stepping off, loading your weight onto one leg then chambering your knee up and kicking downward hitting with the sword of the foot, it can also be done closer range to the inside of the knee, this is more applicable mid fight whereas the first way is an initial strike after a failed strike by your opponent.

Pic 25 - Cover Block and Side Kick to back of knee

Pic 26 - Side Kick to inside of the knee

Kick number 3 is the only kick of the 5 where we say it's better to kick with your shin than your foot. It is a Roundhouse Kick; it can be done lead leg or back leg and to the inner or outer thigh.

For this book we are going to focus on just 1 which will be back leg to outer thigh of they have the same stance as you or a neutral stance or if they have an opposite stance to you it will land to the inner thigh.

To avoid injury, watch how the front foot pivots to allow the other leg to come into range, your shin bone should make contact with the thigh about halfway between the hip and the knee, which is a real sweet spot.

Pic 27 - Close up of the supporting foot pivoting

Pic 28 - Full range shot of the kick landing

Pic 29 - Close up of shin hitting the sweet spot

The 4th Kick is a kick with the inside of the foot to the opponent's shin, you deliver this in the same way you would side foot a Football.

It particularly works well with a clinch and comes from the English system called Purring which is still very popular in rural parts of England. It is worth having a look on YouTube for some videos on Purring.

This Kick can be both painful and unbalancing to set something else up.

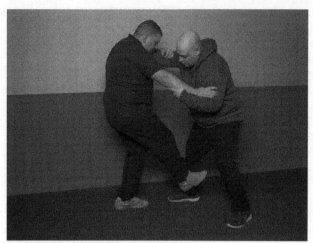

Pic 30 - Purring Kick to the Shin

Kick Number 5 is a Stamp Kick, this can be done to the foot if standing or on the ankle if you get your opponent on the ground.

Pic 31 - Foot stomp from the front

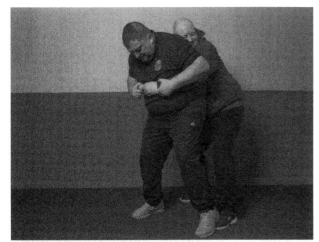

Pic 32 - Foot stomp from rear attack

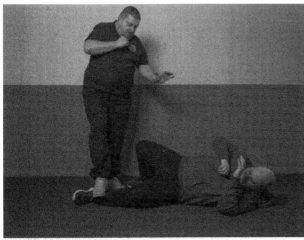

Pic 33 - Stomp to the ankle of a grounded opponent

Pushes

Pushing is a big part of Self Defence, not useless pushing like you see on TV, effective pushing can give you the distance you need to escape or plan your next move like we discussed earlier. There are 2 pushes we will discuss the first one is the Offensive push and the second one is the Defensive push.

The differences are subtle but vital. The Offensive push focuses on moving your opponent the Defensive push is all about moving yourself.

With the offensive push, turn your hips so you have a bit torque to add to your push, then look beyond your attacker to where you want them to be and push.

Pic 34 - Set up of the Offensive push   Pic 35 - Contact on the Offensive push

The defensive push comes because you feel you are not strong enough to push your opponent, so you pit yourself off them to create the space that you need. Practice this against a wall and push yourself off into a good stance and with safe distance.

Pic 36 - Push off your opponent

Pic 37 - Distancing yourself from your opponent after a defensive push

Thumb to Vomit Reflex

The final strike is a very close in strike, if someone has grabbed you very closely you can release yourself from their grip simply by placing your thumb in the Vomit reflex which is in the lower centre part of your throat, it's easier to explain on the pictures, press in then down for a couple of seconds and it should be enough for them to grab their own throat and not you, any longer and you will find out why it got its name.

Pic 38 - Thumb to Vomit reflex

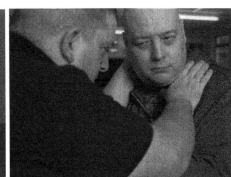
Pic 39 - Close up

Chapter 12
Training for Power, Accuracy & Timing

A lot of these strikes can be very dangerous to do on a training partner as it is all done with no Gloves or Pads so instead, we recommend that you use a variety of Training aids to gain power, accuracy and better timing. Initially they should be trained separately and when you get to a decent level with them then start mixing it up. Here are a few examples

Pic 40 - Palm Strike on a Focus Mitt for Power

Pic 41 - Hammer fist on a Focus Mitt for Power

Pic 42 - Power Slap on a Focus Mitt for Power

Pic 43 - Elbow Strike on a Thai Pad for Power

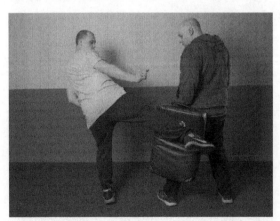

Pic 44 - Roundhouse Kick on a Kick Shield for Power

Pic 45 - Here you see we have taped a Cross to a Punch Bag for Accuracy the Student must try and hit the Cross rather than the big target, this can be done with any piece of equipment and any Strike

Pic 46 - Pad Holder is walking around with the Pad Static this makes it harder to get your accuracy, of course you can add the Cross when you get the hang of it

Pic 47 - Pad Holder throws the Pad towards the Student in order to hit it right your timing needs to be spot on

Pic 48 - Having a Pad holder moving themselves and the pad with a Cross on it covers all 3 aspects Power, Accuracy & Timing.

There are lots of other ways and you can adapt the methods here for different techniques.

Chapter 13
Grappling Techniques

Grappling Techniques are amazing for Self Defence however they are more difficult to learn and without a good level of skill hard to pull off with the adrenaline running wild, but this book would not be complete without showing you a few examples.

The Elbow Scoop

This is a way of turning your opponent or just off balancing them

Pic 49 – Close up of the Elbow Scoop   Pic 50 – The position after Elbow Scoop

Gooseneck Wrist Lock

Wrist's being the smallest joint on the arm is a good place to attack, often it is presented to you on a plate if someone grabs you, this will be shown in chapter 15.

The Basic point is to press the knuckles down so that the wrist is at a more of an acute angle. You also need a secure grip so one arm on either side if the opponent's arm is recommended with both your hands on theirs.

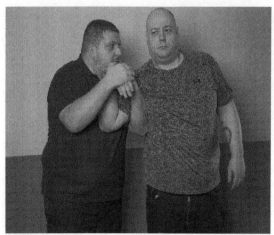

Pic 51 - Gooseneck Wrist Lock

Top Wrist Lock

The Top Wrist Lock is a very dangerous hold that can tear a shoulder or elbow very quickly, there are a few variations and the one I have chosen is the easiest to learn.

Simply grab your opponent's wrist, left to right or right to left. Shoot your other arm through the gap between their arm and torso, adjust your original grip and feed your opponent's wrist towards your other hand, you should now have a two on one grip, pull down on the wrist and lift the elbow.

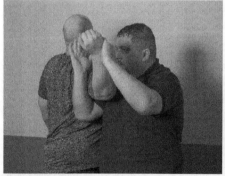

Pic 52 - Set up of the Top Wrist Lock

Pic 53 - Completed Top Wrist Lock

Straight Arm Lock

The straight arm lock is the easiest Grappling Technique to explain. As the name suggests the opponent's arm needs to be straight. Now imagine how you would break a broom handle; you would grab both ends and snap in the middle.

That is how we are going to approach this technique, now you can do this technique from the inside or the outside with slight adjustments.

The key is the Little Finger. You must attack the little finger side. So for the outside Straight Arm Lock you grab your opponent's wrist, turn the arm so the little finger side is pointing towards you, you then step in and push your forearm or ribs into the elbow joint and grab the wrist with both arms now, so the broom handle theory is in play your grab the wrist, the shoulder is connected to the body so you have the security on both ends ready to break the arm in the middle.

The inside technique works in the same way, shoulder is secure already so grab the wrist, turn the arm so the little finger is pointing at you, the main different is you bring your arm underneath to snap the joint. You can also do a downward arm break using the same principle and can be done inside or outside.

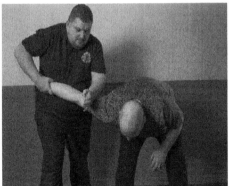 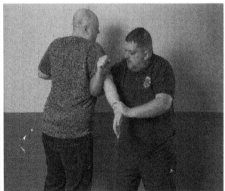

Pic 54 - Straight Arm Lock from outside   Pic 55 - Straight Arm Lock from inside

Hammerlock

The Hammerlock is very practical for restraining but can also be as devastating to the joints as the previous techniques.

Hook your left arm into your opponent's right arm, the crook of the elbow to the crook of the elbow, you then raise their elbow above their shoulder so they do not have the same strength they would have as their arm is in an unnatural position thus giving you the advantage.

Then you crank it down so they are bent forward, step to the outside so they cannot attack your groin.

You can then either restrain them or crank on a bar lock here for a break.

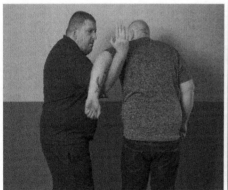

Pic 56 - Hook arm inside your opponent's   Pic 57 - The finished Hammerlock

Face Bar

The next technique in this section is the Face Bar and is attacking a different body part rather than the arm we are now attacking the face and neck. You apply the hold from the rear so you need to get there which we will cover in chapter 15 when we look at full defence scenarios. So, onto the technique, its best to grab first especially if your opponent is taller than you as you will need to either kick their knee or drag back so you can get the required amount of leverage to make the hold successful.

Then when you are in position you need to drive your forearm into the attackers cheek bone and turn the head, this tightens up the neck, then pull them in by pulling your forearm to your chest then secure it by bringing your other arm into play, you do this by punching over their shoulder and then you grab your bicep to secure the lock. You can also connect your hands (as shown)

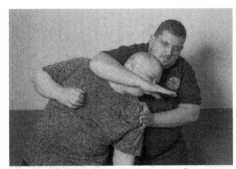 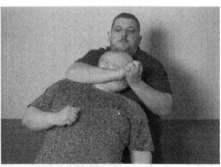

Pic 58 - Turn the head with your forearm   Pic 59 - The finished Face Bar

The Rear Trip

This is the only Takedown I will cover in the book, if someone is a Black Belt in Ju-Jitsu they will know hundreds, but like I have said previously this is a book teaching very Basic Self Defence. So, for the Rear trip grab your opponent Wrist, pull it into you, push on the other shoulder and then put your behind theirs, right to right or left to left going on the same side as the wrist you grabbed. Swoop the leg back and put your opponent on the ground, ideally you want them to fall at your feet, but this requires lots of practice.

Pic 60 - Full shot of the Rear Trip   Pic 61 - Close up of the Rear Trip

Chapter 14
Expedient Weapons

You might wonder what this means, basically an Expedient Weapon is using something you are carrying on you that can be used to aid your Defence. Anything from Keys, Phone, Wallet & Bags can be used as an Expedient Weapon

Keys can be used in close range if someone grabs you then you can scratch your opponent or use it as an enhanced pressure point in a soft area. If you have a bunch of keys, you can flail them at your attacker

Pic 62 - Smashing the bicep with a key to escape

Phones are super valuable and expensive but not as valuable as your life. If you grip your phone and hit someone in the same way you would a hammer fist either to the nose or bicep to release a grip.

Pic 63 - Phone Hammer fist to the Nose   Pic 64 - Phone Hammer fist to the Bicep

Bags are great and depends on the type of bag depends on how best to use them, here are 3 examples. A holdall thrown at someone's feet to unbalance them is a great way to gain some valuable time.

A rucksack can be used as a shield and just like a shield can be used mainly defensively but also offensively.

A handbag swung like the Power Slap is a fantastic expedient Weapon, the handles give you good range and the amount of stuff kept in there makes it a great impact Weapon.

Pic 65 - Throwing a bag to the legs   Pic 66 - Using a Bag as a Shield

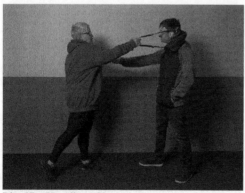

Pic 67 - Handbag Slap

Of course, there is many more especially if you are indoors, they were just some obvious examples.

Chapter 15
Defences against 10 common attacks

For the final chapter of Section 1 I want to show a defence against 10 common attacks using the Skills you have learnt in the earlier chapters of the book.

It is important to know these are not the only defences against these attacks, just 1 example, there is so many different ways and depends totally on how they attack, their size and so many other factors.

It's important to remember these 3 words, Adapt, Apply & Create

Adapt to the scenario and situation
Apply the skills and knowledge you have
Create your response from what they give you.

These are the 10 common attacks I chose, again there are much more, we are not even scratching the surface as this book does not cover Ground defences, Weapon Defences, Defences against Multiple Attackers and other Adverse Situations.

Attack 1 - Swinging Punch

Pic 68 - Two people square off

Pic 69 – Smother Block - Swinging Punch

Pic 70 - Defender applies an Elbow

Pic 71 - The follow up strike is a Knee to the stomach

Pic 72 - Followed by a Push Away

Pic 73 - Defender walking away with their Fence up

Attack 2 - Straight Punch

Pic 74 - Two people square off

Pic 75 - Defender moves outside of the punch and applies a cover block

Pic 76 - Defender throws a swift Side kick to the knee

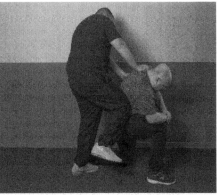

Pic 77 - Defender uses a round knee to the ribs

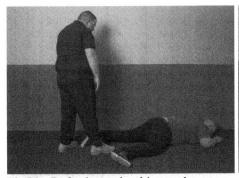

Pic 78 - Defender pushes his attacker over

Pic 79 - Defender stamps on the ankle

Attack 3 - Swinging Kick

Pic 80 - Two people square off

Pic 81 - Attacker swings his leg in a football kick Defender step off on a capital letter Y step

Pic 82 – Pivot and clinch the head

Pic 83 – Knee strike to stomach

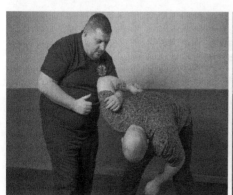

Pic 84 – Set up the Hammerlock

Pic 85 - Secure Hammerlock and apply additional pressure to the wrist

Attack 4 - Two Handed Grab

Pic 86 - Attacker Grabs the throat

Pic 87 - Kick to the shin to soften the grip

Pic 88 - Step back and do a wedging block

Pic 89 - Follow up with a Palm Strike

Pic 90 - Defender then clinches

Pic 91 - Then finishes with the Rear Trip

Attack 5 - Single Hand Lapel Grab

Pic 92 - Attacker Grabs the lapel

Pic 93 - Defender covers the Grabbing Arm with their Left Hand

Pic 94 - Defender applies the Power Slap

Pic 95 - Defender punches his arm through the opponents arm and torso setting up the next move

Pic 96 - Circle your wrist re grab your opponent's wrist

Pic 97 - Feed the attacking arm up to Top Wrist Lock

Attack 6 - Single Hand Throat Grab

Pic 98 - Attacker Grabs the Defender's Throat

Pic 99 - Defender bends the attacking arm with their forearm

Pic 100 - As the Attacker is close apply a Hammer fist to the nose

Pic 101 - Followed by an Elbow Strike

Pic 102 – Set up a Finger Grab

Pic 103 – Break the attackers' fingers (at least 2)

Attack 7 - Old School Head Lock

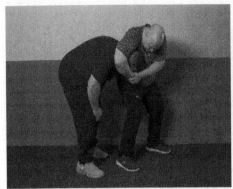

Pic 104 - Attacker Grabs the Defender in a head lock

Pic 105 - Defender hammer fists the closest thigh

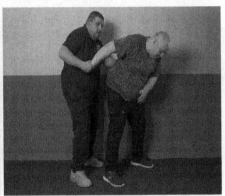

Pic 106 - Defender pushes the opponents away

Pic 107 - Defender grabs attackers' wrist

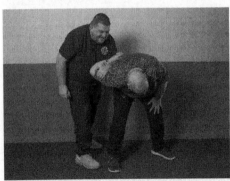

Pic 108 - Defenders applies a Hammerlock

Pic 109 - Then transitions to the Face Bar

Attack 8 - Pull Head Down & Grab Neck

Pic 110 - Attacker grabs the defenders head

Pic 111 - Attacker grabs around the defenders' neck with a guillotine

Pic 112 - Defender strikes the attackers Groin

Pic 113 - Defender grabs attackers' wrist with a two on one and releases the grip

Pic 114 - Defender stands up straight and goes under the attacker's arm

Pic 115 - Defender performs the Outside Arm Break

Attack 9 - Under Arm Bear Hug

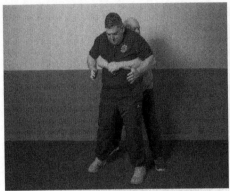

Pic 116 - Attacker grabs the defender from behind with an Under Arm Bear Hug

Pic 117 - Defender hits back of attackers hand with a single knuckle strike

Pic 118 - Defender shoots their arm inside the grip of their opponents to create space

Pic 119 - Defender throws a back elbow to the Head

Pic 120 - Defender fully breaks the grip & turns to face and clinches the neck

Pic 121 - The defender delivers a knee strike to the stomach

Attack 10 - Over Arm Bear Hug

Pic 122 - Attacker grabs the defender from behind with an Over Arm Bear Hug

Pic 123 - Defender stamps on the attackers' foot

Pic 124 - Defender steps forward with one foot

Pic 125 - The elbows the attacker in the stomach

Pic 126 – Defender performs Takedown

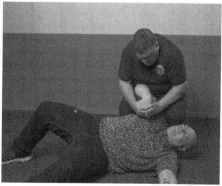

Pic 127 – Followed by Wrist Lock

Pic 128 – Me teaching Self Defence at the UK Martial Arts Show
(Photo credit Nickie Johnson)

Section 2
Specific Female Self Defence

Chapter 16
What makes Women's Self Defence different to Men's?

Although this is aimed at Women these chapters are also important for Men to read as we all have Women in our lives that we love, care for and want to protect and reading this book will give you a better understanding of Female Self Defence and you can pass this information on to your loved ones.

So, I felt compelled to do to write a few chapters for Women's Self Defence as it is very different, now how is it different you might say, now a Woman versus Woman isn't that much different than a man versus man but there are still differences, the main difference is really when it comes to man attacking a Woman.

So, it's important to know strengths and weaknesses and if you can't get past this bit you may end up out of your depth.

Most Women are not as strong as Men, not all but generally they weigh less and are shorter and care less for muscle mass.

Most Women take longer to act violently than men, again most not all.

If you fit into any of those categories, then the next few chapters are important to you.

By understanding that a male attacker may be stronger, bigger etc will mean that you will use better tactics if a confrontation becomes violent. This may offend some people, but I like to think by pointing this out it will help more than it offends.

Some Women can flick the violence switch quicker than others, in my Martial Arts School I have trained many Females including over a Dozen World Champions, they can spar with the men and give as good as it gets and could pull off kicks in the street I would not recommend most people try, that is basically for two reasons, the first being they are well trained and second because they had something inside them that attracted them to Kick Boxing, Martial Arts etc. A constant theme of this book is that it is not the well-trained Ninja's that I am aiming this book at.

A major difference between men and women is their psychology. A man can flick the violent switch really quickly if you say something about them but a Woman may not be the same, however if you switch it up and get them to imagine that something has said something about a loved one you quickly see the lioness escape out of them as women are a lot more selfless and care more for others than themselves more often than not.

If a married couple are watching TV and something gory comes on the male would probably enjoy it and the female may turn away or hide behind a cushion. So, it's important to understand something so simple like that so that you can overcome the reluctance to use force, because if you don't understand the psychology behind it, you cannot begin to understand it.

If you feel like an attacker is about to go violent you need to go from Lady to Lioness really quick, to trigger this imagine that someone is doing something nasty to another female in your life mother, sister, daughter, best friend etc, that is the quickest way you will overcome the reluctance to become Violent and unless the Lioness quick enough to save yourself.

Male attackers are less likely to throw a punch, they don't want a fight, it is often some sort of reward they are after either sexual or something like a bag snatch, knowing this gives you an advantage, it gives you something to prepare for. They are more likely to grab which means you can prepare by striking your way out of the situation.

Chapter 17
A Woman's best Weapons

Now we understand how Female Self Defence works it is important to start looking at the best things to do if you are in a confrontation.

In chapter 11 we discussed striking techniques, all of these are relevant to female Self Defence. Slap, Palm & Hammer is a good thing to have in your head.

Women naturally slap better than Men so it's a good place to start, so when you get the technically side of the power slap down you have a great technique in your arsenal.

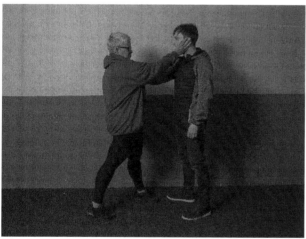

Pic 129 - Power Slap

Palm Strikes work really well, Women do not want to be close, and a palm strike is quite long range and can put distance between you and your attacker if they grab, which is the most likely attack.

Hammer fists are much better for everyone but certainly for Women due to the smaller bones in their hands.

Elbows & Knees are also great for Women, what they lack in power they make up for Women having more pointy bones, these can really do some damage.

The best kicks out of the ones mentioned are the front kick to groin, side kick to knee and foot stomp. All of these strikes are covered in the technique's sections earlier in the book.

Pushes are obviously great especially the defensive push and of course the Vomit Reflex requires no power at all so that's a good one.

Pic 130 - Defensive Push (start)   Pic 131 - Defensive Push (finish)

And of course, the Fence & Guard work very well, here you can communicate that you are confident or even that you have friend or partner around the corner or be compliant if it's a reward such as a phone or money that they desire.

The Grappling techniques are not the best things to use if a male is attacking you as they are likely to have a size and strength advantage, so you are best sticking to the Hit and Move principle.

So, what else do we have. First of all is the Face Wash, this is a great technique and involves the defender quickly and constantly dragging their fingers down their attacker's face, although not massively painful it can be distracting and discomforting and buy you some time for a follow up or escape.

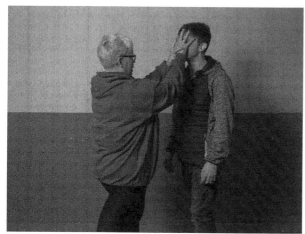

Pic 133 - The Face Wash

We talked about targets in the Striking section earlier in the book, for women it is the same but here is something to remember. Eyeballs and Low Balls! They are great targets; you cannot build muscle around them. A good strike in those will make your getaway easier.

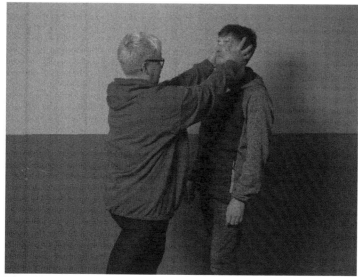

Pic 133 - Eye Gouge

Pic 134 - Groin Kick

Other important things to note are if you Drop your weight, you are harder to lift or move around, so training that can be very beneficial, having a good stance could mean the difference between a successful defence and not so successful one.

Hair comes into play a lot more in confrontations involving Females, that's male attackers and female attackers. If someone grabs your hair, it's important to get them off as soon as possible because if you have long hair, it can be very painful and a very good handle.

Now if you slap them and knock them out you could end up with a huge chunk of hair missing or could end up being dragged to the floor. So, think about the grabbing hand, secure it first, if you do this with one hand you can still strike if you use two hands you can step back until the grip is released.

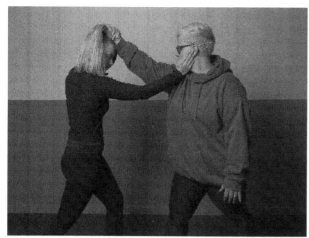
Pic 135 - Single Handed control and slap

Pic 136 - Two handed pull down

Finally shouting is an important Weapon for you, someone is more likely to come to a woman's aid than a man's. Help, fire, rape are short words that can be instantly recognisable that someone is in danger. Help is obvious, fire although misleading is still a good thing to shout, people will always look if they hear fire and if they see instead a female being attacked, I'm sure they will understand, rape obviously should be used with caution if someone is starting a sexual assault then it is the right word to shout.

Chapter 18
Advice on Domestic Violence

So, this one is a touchy subject and there for it will be our smallest chapter however I felt that it must be covered.

Nobody has a right to inflict mental or physical pain on another person not even your Husband, especially not your Husband. There is no excuse for it.

If you are attacked in your home cover up, push away and escape. Do not be afraid to tell someone who loves you, it could start off where you think it's not too bad and can handle but can easily escalate and become acceptable to you both, but it is not.

Pic 137 - Ladies Guard

Chapter 19
Dealing with Unwanted Attention

This is a part of the book which could be massive, unwanted attention can be just a guy who hits on you in a club, it could also lead to stalking and even to a Sexual Assault.

If someone won't leave you alone, you need to make it clear that you are not interested. If it gets physical, for example if they grab you then you must hit back straight away, now by that I mean just release the grip and create distance, if they have grabbed you then they have chosen when it went physical, you have no alternative than to hit back.

Now this can go one way or the other, they could leave you alone, but things could also escalate. In the next few sequences, I will show you releases that are not too aggressive and should not escalate the situation but there are no guarantees, everyone is an individual.

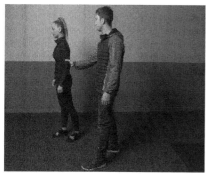 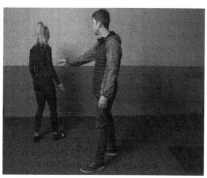

Example 1
Pic 138 - Attacker Grabs the back of the arm

Pic 139 - Turn 180 degrees

Pic 140 - Walk away

Example 2
Pic 142 - Attacker Grabs your Wrist (straight)

Pic 143 – Close up of turning the arm and pull through between thumb and index finger

Pic 144 – Arm is now ready to pull through between thumb and index finger and walk away

Chapter 20
Sexual Assaults

For this chapter I really want to give some advice on how to defend yourself in the worst possible position.

At first there are things you need to know.

1/ There are many opportunities for you to make a move, you don't fall onto the floor naked. Your attacker has to try and undress you in order to get what they want from you. This may seem obvious but is often not told to you, this is where you have opportunities to strike.

2/ Unless they are a skilled Wrestler, and most attackers of this nature are not then they won't land in the right position. This again is your chance to strike.

3/ If they take you to the ground, they will want to break their fall by putting their hands owt as they land, you can avoid heavy impact with the ground by hugging onto their back, then when you both land you have the opportunity to strike first.

Fear will hit you in this situation so it's important to keep the advice and techniques I'm going to give you very basic.

So first of all, let's look at Targets. Due to the closeness of the Attack the eyes are a great target, on courses we have said this numerous times and often its net with…. Oh, I couldn't do that! Well, this guy wants to rape you so you need to get your head around it, fingers to the eyes are one of the best things you can do from here.

Second target is the groin. Whether it's a punch, grab, knee or kick this is a real sweet spot for men. They cannot build muscle around either of these areas and they are the most painful.

Another target is the neck and throat, jamming your fingers in there can be quite painful to a person especially if you can find the Carotid Sinus and Vomit Reflex.

Now let's look at your Weapons. Women tend to have strong legs which you can use to kick, push and squeeze.

Squeezing can be holding an arm or leg where you want it and kicking and pushing will be the techniques that will give you the distance you need to get up and escape.

Pointy bits! Elbows & Knees, women tend to have pointy elbows & Knees so these can be utilised very well as close in you can grind these into your attacker for pain and discomfort which can give you separation from them to deliver powerful strikes or mount an escape.

Nipping & Scratching. It's not pleasant but nor is what they have planned. Nipping into sensitive areas can really help unbalance them again and as always, the goal is to create distance and separation for your escape.

Of course, with us using the word Weapon if there is anything nearby you can use to aid your defence then do it. Now let's look at a typical scenario.

Pic 144 - Defender hooking on as attacker takes them down so they are not injured on the way down

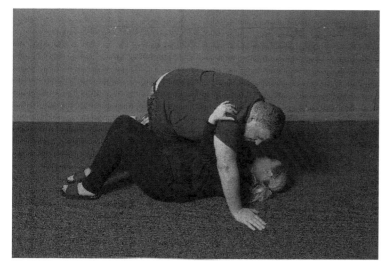

Pic 145 - Attacker landed on the side of the Defender

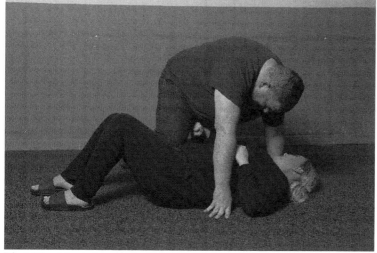

Pic 146 - Attack the Groin as they try and move to a better position

Striking Areas

These next 6 pictures will show 6 ways of striking or pushing away from on the ground.

Pic 147 - Pushing back via the Eyes

Pic 148 - Attacking the Carotid Sinus

Pic 149 - Attacking the Vomit Reflex

Pic 150 - Grinding the Elbow in

Pic 151 - Kicking from on your back

Pic 152 - Pushing away using your Legs

Worst Case Scenario

Even in this situation you still have a chance to escape by employing any of the above strikes and working on the principles mentioned. If they attack you they are likely to be clothed still and you are, to undress someone from here if they are in trousers is extremely difficult and even in a skirt with underwear they have to pull your underwear down and then at some point move themselves back, there you have yet another chance to strike, then when they are undressing this is another opportunity, even if they are using 1 hand and controlling you with the other, they are not strong enough and won't be focused enough to hold you down if you employ the tactics we have just talked about.

There are windows of time to strike, YOU just have to recognise them and unleash hell on them. The deserve it, it's never your fault.

So here is some common advice for every situation when it comes to Ladies Self Defence

1/ Do not walk far alone especially at night and don't take short cuts
2/ Don't go anywhere with someone you do not know
3/ Always make sure someone knows where you are going
4/ Keep your mobile phone charged
5/ Have something like a thick pen, keys, phone or handbag on you to help aid your defence
6/ Make lots of noise if you feel threatened
7/ Do not let anyone put their hands on you, nobody has that right
8/ If you're in your car alone, lock the doors
9/ Remember your Weapons & Targets
10/ Unleash the Lioness! Do whatever it takes to survive the situation

Section 3
Children's Self Defence

Chapter 21
Building Confidence & Skills

The key to unlocking a Childs ability to defend themselves is undoubtably confidence, there for the biggest recommendation I can give you is to enrol your Child in Martial Arts classes.

They are renowned for building Confidence as well as other important attributes such as Self Discipline, Focus and Respect.

They will also learn valuable techniques and skills that will help them develop the confidence to defend themselves if the need ever arises.

This is the firm base required for your Child to not only learn to Defend themselves but also have the Confidence to actually stand up for themselves and the morals and ethics of when to use these skills.

Pic 153 - Confident Child

So, let's break down what situations a child might find them self in.

First of all, an actual Fight, we define this by it being a child a similar age and size, we call this School Fights and has been happening in the playgrounds for many years.

Then we have Bullying, which is usually a bigger or older child and makes it harder to fight back.

Finally, we have Strangers which are adults or much older Children. The techniques they use are much different to the other two.

Each of these 3 aspects will have a dedicated Chapter later in this book but first let's look at techniques Children should learn in order to be able to defend themselves in these different situations.

Chapter 22
Techniques all Children should know

Out of the 5 chapters on Children's Self Defence this is the main one for the actual techniques and will be more picture based than the other Chapters.

In this chapter we will cover Essential skills and techniques such as Pushes, Restraints, Trips & Strikes

First up pushing. Now this may seem like common sense, which it is and that is what makes it an Essential Skill for Kids. Pushing comes into all 3 aspects which is Fights, Bullying & Strangers. It can be utilised in all 3 equally well but in different ways.

When you push you must have a strong base, as Dave Turton says, "you can't fire a cannon from a canoe" and this is never truer than when pushing.

We have two main pushes, the offensive and defensive push. The offensive push is every day push away but the defensive push is one utilised against someone bigger, with this it's almost like a rewind where you put your bent arms on your attacker and push back

Pic 154 - The Offensive Push (normal)

Pic 155 – The Defensive Push (start)   Pic 156 - The Defensive Push (finish)

Restrains work differently depends on the situation. Like any technique they can work in any environment but restraints are much better against people around your own size, once you get them into position you can hold someone stronger but it can be difficult to get into those restraints against a stronger person, therefor you may need to do Softening Strikes . in order to escalate your position.

Restraints are best used in the "School Fights" section, they are especially useful in a situation where you are not wanting to be "in trouble" or perceived as the Bully when someone picks a fight with you.

As this is the Children's section we will focus on the best restraints for Children.

Hammerlock

Pic 157 – Start

Pic 158 – Detail

Pic 159 - Finish

129

Gooseneck

Pic 160 - Start

Pic 161 - Detail

Pic 162 - Finish

Double Wrist Lock

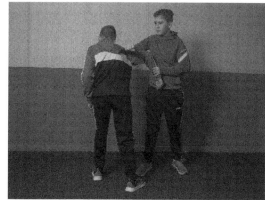

Pic 163 - Start

Pic 164 - Detail

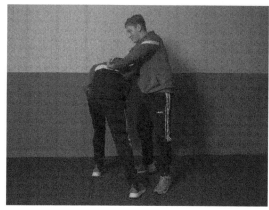

Pic 165 - Finish

131

Long Wrist Lock

Pic 166 - Start

Pic 167 – Detail

Pic 168 - Finish

Arm Lever

Pic 169 - Start

Pic 170 - Detail

Pic 171 - Finish

133

The main Trips we are looking at are adaptions of Reap techniques from Ju-Jitsu.

So, we are going to categorise as Outside Trip and Inside Trip.

First up the Outside Trip, this is similar to the Osoto Gari or Major Outer Reap. The key is to get your leg behind your attackers and at the right time push them back to unbalance them allowing your leg to trip them. For the best result you should go right leg behind right leg or left leg behind left leg. Stamping back will bend the leg and aid the defence better than swinging the leg like in Ju-Jitsu, especially against a stronger opponent, with everything you do there is a minimum and maximum effect, the minimum effect is that you unbalance your opponent enough to escape or get in a strike and in this case the maximum is that your opponent ends up on the ground.

This principle is the same for the Inside Trip also. The difference here is that your right leg is attacking your opponents inside leg leg or vice versa. On this technique you are hooking in and pulling your opponent's leg forward whilst you push. This is particularly effective if you are shorter than your opponent.

Outside Trip

Pic 172 - Start

Pic 173 - Detail

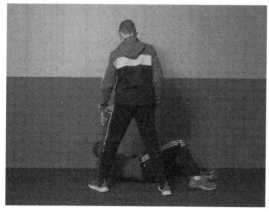

Pic 174 - Finish

Inside Trip

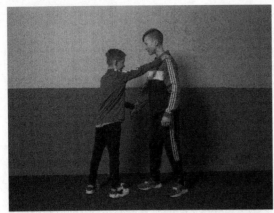

Pic 175 - Start

Pic 176 - Detail

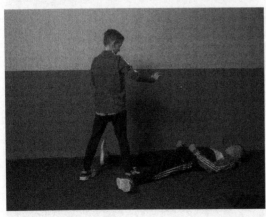

Pic 177 - Finish

Finally, we have Strikes. The theme of this book is the essential stuff, the basics and just a few things to learn that will stay in your head. So, we will start with long range techniques which are of course kicks. The kicks have two important elements, the part of the leg you hit with and the target.

We are just going to focus on 3 kicks first, they are the first 3 kicks you learn in most Martial Arts but adapted for Self Defence. As they are long range strikes, they are specifically useful against larger attackers as it can keep the range long.

First of all, the front kick, this can be a kick to the shin or knee with the bottom of foot or toes with a strong shoe or a shin to the groin.

Both of these Kicks are used mainly against larger attackers as they can be dangerous against other Children. The goal of these Kicks is to escape from an adult attacker.

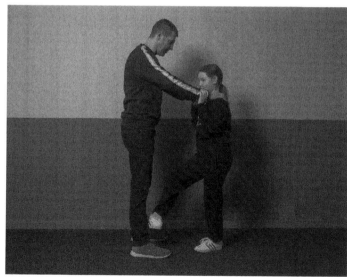

Pic 178 - Kick to shin

Pic 179 - Kick to groin

Next up is the side kick to the knee, again this is for escape from an adult attacker. It can be to the inside or outside of the knee and you kick with the bottom of the foot.

Pic 180 - Side Kick to the outside of the knee

Pic 181 - Side Kick to the inside of the knee

The final kick is the low round kick with the shin to the thigh. Now this one takes more training than the other two and you should seek tuition to get it right.

Pic 182 - Inside leg kick

Pic 183 - Outside leg kick

Moving onto medium range we have strikes with the Hand. The theme of the strikes is that it's against larger opponents to escape and this is no different.

Even an accomplished junior Kick Boxing Champion will struggle to hurt a grown man with punches, and you are more likely to hurt your own hand, which is not ideal in these situations, so I recommend the use of the Palm Strike & Hammer Fist.

First up the Palm strike, the aim here is to hit with the heel of the hand to your attackers nose, therefor a hard weapon to a soft target, this should mean the eyes water and the nose bleeds if you connect correctly, another of Dave's saying is "you can't fight if you can't see" so this is the opportunity to escape. Hit and run again being the theme.

With the Hammer fist it's the same target the nose but also you can use it to break a grip by targeting the forearms, biceps and thighs in order to escape.

The key is to make a strong fist like you would a punch but instead of using the Knuckles you use the bottom of the fist in the same way you would hammer a nail into a wall hence the name

Pic 184 - Palm Strike

Pic 185 - Hammer fist to nose

Pic 186 - Hammer fist to biceps against a grab

Finally, we have Close Range strikes that we only use if your attacker has closed the range by grabbing or pinning. These include but are not limited to elbows, knees & stamps.

So first of all, Elbows, first let's look at the strengths and weaknesses. The strengths are that it's a powerful strike and elbows can be pointy and sharp and can often cut the opponent open. It's also quite versatile and can be a forward strike, downward strike or rear strike and can hit various targets. The downside is the lack of range and that is why we use it close in, so it's important to know this.

Pic 187 - Elbow strike to the face

Pic 188 - Rear elbow to the stomach

Pic 189 - Downward elbow to the arm

Knees have the same attributes powerful and sharp but only for use close range which is why we included them in this section. The best targets go from the stomach down to the groin and then the thigh. These can-do serious damage to your attacker and especially if you are targeting low can increase your chances of escape.

Pic 190 - Knee strike to the stomach

Pic 191 - Knee strike to the groin to create separation

Pic 192 - Knee to the thigh

Stamps are the final techniques, this is just basically stamping on the foot but can also be to the shin, I have also included the rear swing kick if your attacker has picked you up and cannot stamp

Pic 193 - Stamp against rear bear hug

Pic 194 - Stamp against throat grab from the front (pinned)

Pic 195 - Stamp to the shin

Pic 196 - Swinging kick if picked up

145

Chapter 23
School Fights

Now let's start this chapter by saying that we are not encouraging Children fighting at school, but it does happen and it's important to look at ways to defend yourself if you did get into a fight.

This is a book on Self Defence and if a child gets in a fight, they must defend themselves, if that means getting away, fighting back or defending until its split up then you must be prepared.

Often fights at School or even out of school are reasonably well matched and more often than not in front of a crowd. These fights tend not to have a winner as they are often broken up. In this chapter we will show you ways to protect yourself in this situation by showing defences against common attacks

Swinging Punch - Duck Under and push away

Pic 197 - Duck under the punch   Pic 198 - Push them from behind

Swinging Punch - Smother Block, Knee, Double Wrist Lock

Pic 199 - Smother Block   Pic 200 – Knee Strike

Pic 201 - Set up the Double Wrist Lock   Pic 202 - Apply the Double Wrist Lock

Swinging Punch - Smother Block, Knee Strike & Rear Trip

Pic 203 - Smother Block

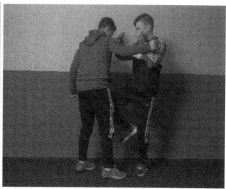
Pic 204 – Knee Strike

Pic 205 - Leg Positioning for Rear Trip

Pic 206 - Takedown

Two Handed Grab - Step back and open hands and palm strike

Pic 207 - The Grab and start position of defence

Pic 208 - Step back and open hands

Pic 209 - Palm Strike to the Face

Single Handed Grab - Bend arm and Elbow Strike

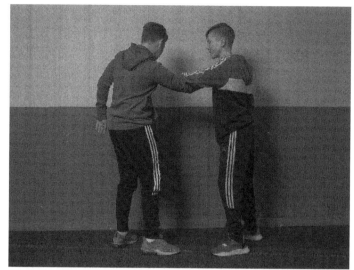

Pic 210 - Attacker Grabs and defender bends the arm

Pic 211 – Elbow Strike

Head Lock - Hammer fist the leg, grip the wrist and stand up into Hammerlock

Pic 212 - Head Lock position

Pic 213 - hammer fist the thigh

Pic 214 - Grab the wrist

Pic 215 - Put their arm up their back in a Hammerlock

Bear Hug - Stamp, drop weight, elbow, step forward and kick the knee

Pic 216 - Stamp on the foot

Pic 217 - Drop weight

Pic 218 - step forward

Pic 219 - kick to the knee

Kicked on the Ground - Cover and bring your legs into play

Pic 220 - Cover up against a kick

Pic 221 - Scoot round

Pic 222 - Now you have your legs in between you and your attackers you can kick their legs

Pic 223 - Safely Stand up

These are just a few of the many different attacks & defence situations.

Chapter 24
Dealing with Bullying

Nobody has a right to Bully you and you don't have a right to Bully anyone else. That's a statement we tell our Kids in class. Unfortunately, it does happen though and is every School around the World.

There are lots of different types of Bullying including mental, emotional & physical and lots of different ways someone can be bullied such as Cyber, Text or in person.

As this is a book on Self Defence we are focusing on the Physical aspect. However, I just want to offer a bit of advice on the other aspects. First of all, for Kids, you must always tell someone, the bully tells you not to because they are scared of what will happen if you do, so always tell a parent or teacher or any adult that you trust and always be open with your parents with your phone, social media etc. Never accept friend requests or messages from any one you don't know, even if it's a child as it might now be. You have no idea who you are actually talking too.

The best Advice for Parents I can give is to be a good listener, being open with your Child will make them feel more comfortable talking to you. If you notice a difference in their behaviour this could be down to something happening at School and that could be Bullying. This is when you should ask if everything is ok, it may take a few times for them to say what's going off so please persevere, if you still think somethings happening then you can ask someone else to talk to them, like an older sibling, cool auntie or uncle or someone outside of family and of course asking the teacher to help is always a good thing.

One thing to remember is that Bullying happens at the earliest stages of Primary School and also at High School. It needs to stop or that can be a lot of trauma for your Child over a long period of time that will affect them all the way through their Life.

I mentioned Confidence earlier, Kids tend to Bully due to lack of confidence and this could be down to having some form of bullying themselves or to make them feel good in front of people, that in itself shows a lack of confidence that they need the approval of others.

So, we go back to the first Chapter of the Children's section of this book and discuss Confidence. Being confident under the scariest of situations can be amongst the most powerful things you can do. You don't have to call out the bully just something simple like saying "leave me alone" or "I'm not scared of you" clearly with confidence could mean they start doubting themselves.

Also having skills and the confidence to use them can be very off putting to a Bully. By this I mean something simple like being able to release someone's grip on you makes them wonder what else you know.

If the situations escalates then some of the techniques, you have learnt in Chapter 22 & 23 need to be employed.

The best tactic or principle that I can recommend is Move Hit Move. Often Bullies are bigger, so you don't want to be hit or grabbed by them, so that's the first move. Followed by Hit, this could be a strike, push, foot stamp or whatever it takes to create distance. The final word is once again move and this is your escape. Now the word escape is important as just getting away is not enough. Get away and tell someone what has happened.

Pic 224 - Typical physical bullying picture

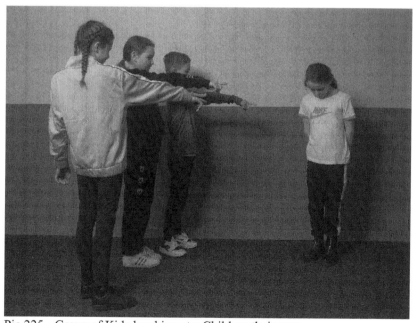

Pic 225 - Group of Kids laughing at a Child on their own

159

Chapter 25
Stranger Danger

One of the scariest parts of being a parent is knowing there are terrible people in this world that would do mental, physical & emotional harm to Children.

When you first have a child, they are with you 24/7, as they grow so does their circle of space. At first being in another room watching TV, then its playing in the Garden, then playing on the street and then going to the park with friends and so on.

Depends on the area you live in, and beliefs of the parent depends on when these happen but eventually as Kids get older, they start getting more freedom. So as parents you need to prepare them for this.

Start by explaining that Stranger Danger happens at all stages of a Childs Development. Younger children are abducted for different reasons to teenagers and remember abductions happen to adults too. Nobody is safe and it's hard to get into the mind of someone who would do this as their mind is very different to our own. There is no rational reason why anyone would want to harm or abduct a Child, but the fact is that it does happen.

So here are a few lessons children must know in order to be a bit safer

1/ You never ever go with a Stranger. There is never a reason to do this. Strangers will take 1 of 2 options to lure you in with words. The first one is do you want to come and see my puppy or would you like some sweets. Both of these can be appealing to a child and its down to the parent to talk to them about it and explain that if they go with a Stranger, they may not ever see their Family again, now this might seem like you're scaring them but its education and important to know.

2/ The other way of a Stranger luring a Child into their car is by saying Parents have asked me to pick you up. So, it's important to tell them that you would never send a stranger to pick you up and go through a list of 5 people who may pick them up from School or elsewhere if you the parent could not get them. This would include Grandparents, Aunties, Uncles, Older Siblings, Family Friends or their friends Parents. You should be able to make a list or between 3 and 5 people there to put their mind at ease and make them understand, children can be easily lead so having fact-based answers will help a lot.

3/ Speaking of the word Answers, you never have to actually answer a stranger. Yes, its rude to not speak when spoken to but the exception is when it's a stranger. If you speak to them, it gives them chance to grab or make a move.

4/ Do not take sweets from strangers ever! I'm sure if you tell your parents, you have refused sweets from a Stranger, they will buy you some themselves. What you think are sweets may not be and if you take something that could be drugs you will not have your wits about you and won't be able to control the situation.

5/ If a stranger grabs you then you must make as much noise as possible and make other people around you aware that this isn't your parent and you're not just having a strop. Shout clear words, HELP is obvious but always the best first choice FIRE although is misleading gets attention, if you do get someone's attention this is where shouting help comes in or clearly shouting "this is not my mum" or "this is not my dad" this can get the attention and help you need or just scare the stranger off

7/ Moving onto the next tip. Strangers can be both Women & Men. If you are reading this book and imaging the attacker its natural to think of a man, however that's not always the case, women are just as likely to be Strangers as men

8/ That goes nicely onto the next tip which is safe people and safe places. Running away is not always the most valid form of Self Defence, where are you running too? How do you know you can outrun your attacker?

164

So where is a safe place or person. A safe place is your friend's house which is close to where you are and closer than home, same with a family member, shops are safe places, usually a shop is occupied by more than one person, and you can call home from there. Stopping to ask a Mum with 2 children if you can use their phone is safer than asking some teenagers down an alley. So, it takes some judgement on the child's part and with good advice from parent they can work out where is best to go if home is too far. Remember we are talking about older Children here generally Teenagers. For younger Children it might be that you're playing on the street and a stranger pulls up in their car, you and all your friends go to the nearest of your houses and tell someone straight away, for a really young Child who might just be in their garden they should run straight back in the house, don't shout or it might make the stranger panic and grab you.

9/ If you think you are being followed then get out your phone ring someone, just by telling someone where you are means that person can come and find you and could make your attacker think twice, also you can say I'm going into so and so's house round the corner to wait for you even if you don't know anyone that lives close it might just make them think twice.

10/ If all else fails and you have been grabbed it's time to go physical

Pic 226 - Groin Kick

Here are some examples of very dangerous situations children may find themselves in

Pic 227 - Stranger talking to a Child

Pic 228 - Stranger trying drag a child into their car

Pic 229 - Child being followed down an alley

Final Thoughts

Congratulations! You are now a White Belt in Self Defence.

The goal of the book is to introduce you to some basic principles of Self Defence, to raise awareness and to inspire the Nation to get involved in some sort of Self Defence training. This will truly make the world a safer place.

Everyone deserves to be able to live their life with as little fear as possible.

This book is about the absolute basics of Self Defence. There are so many other amazing books that go deep into things like Facing Fear and how your mind works in these situations by the likes of Geoff Thompson & Rory Miller. Both of whom I've trained with and are extremely knowledgeable. There are so many things I have not covered as I think its things you should get from actual Tuition such as being attacked by Multiple people, defences against Weapons, defences in Adverse Situations such as on the ground, seated, on stairs etc. Again, something you should get from training.

That is my biggest recommendation, join a class and learn Self Defence. It's also great for socialising and getting proper instruction in Self Defence is one the best way you can spend your spare time.

This book is aimed at everyone, it's not for Martial Arts Instructors who have taught for many years, you guys know this stuff, you can teach this and can certainly defend yourselves.

I want this book to be something that is in every household as it covers the entire family and the whole idea is educate on the basics of Self Defence and inspire more people to take lessons. If you try any of these moves in this book, please take care to not hurt yourself or your partner, hence why I recommend gaining Tuition.

I hope you enjoyed reading it as much as I enjoyed writing it.

These are some of the students who have spent the most time learning Self Defence systems under me.

Pic 239 – Some of my SDF Modern Street Combat Black Belts taken in 2016
Back Row: Gavin Collins, Martin McAteer, Mick Woodhall, Elaine Simmonds, Dave Wortley, Alan Orwin & Carl Spilman
Front Row: Paul Bell, Tommy Long, Me, Jon Glarvey & Stefan Johnson

Pic 231 – Another SDF Modern Street Combat Black Belts with Master Dave Turton taken 2021
Back Row: Stefan Johnson, Adam Wheatley, Paul Neilson, Mick Woodhall & Mary Doyle
Front Row: Dave Turton, Jon Glarvey, Angela Sockett, Gavin Collins & Me

Afterword

The techniques in this book will be backed up with videos on our YouTube Channel also named Essential Self Defence.

And for any more information please email andy.acmac@yahoo.co.uk

If you enjoyed this book look out for my 2nd Book coming out late 2022/early 2023 called "The Wonderful World of Martial Arts"

Printed in Great Britain
by Amazon